Dear Single Mom

YOU WERE BUILT TO DEFY THE ODDS

Stories Compiled by

ALANDRIA LLOYD

ISBN: 978-1-7360573-3-9

Contents

Introduction

"I did not sign up for this!!!"

"How will we ever survive?"

"Can I do this on my own?!?"

Those are just a few thoughts that swim around in single mothers' minds at least once during their journey of raising children alone. They are often overlooked, misjudged, and forgotten, not only by the fathers of their children but also by society. Single moms are often frowned upon and look down on, but no more!

"Dear Single Mom" is a compilation of survival stories written by single mothers to shift perspectives, destroy false narratives, and empower others experiencing similar circumstances.

The women in this book exude grace, strength, and power as they boldly share their testimonies in hopes of inspiring and empowering other single mothers. They didn't allow a status to define them, and now they are coming together to root for and push other moms to the finish line throughout this marathon called "life."

1

Not a Harlequin Romance

I still remember the day that I found out I was going to be a single mother. It was February 15, 1996. The reason that date stands out in my mind is because it was the day after Valentine's Day. I was seven months pregnant when my baby's father informed me that he no longer wanted our relationship. There was no real explanation except that he said, "I'm just not feeling it anymore." Those words were imprinted into my mind. I was stunned and so hurt.

I couldn't find the words to even ask him why. My pride would not allow me to give him all of the reasons why we should stay together. My heart broke into a million pieces that day. The vision of being a happily married couple with the white picket fence raising our children together was shattered. Looking back on the days that led up to that moment, I probably should have seen it coming. As my belly grew bigger, his attitude towards me began to change. He became less affectionate and less attentive. He was irritable and more distant as my pregnancy progressed. This behavior was, of course, a great contrast from the way he treated me in the beginning of our relationship.

I want to take you back to the day we met. I was a freshman in college, adjusting to my newfound freedom and the excitement of becoming a woman. Leaving my mother's house and moving on to the college campus was really scary at first. Living under my mom's strict rules always gave me the desire to get out on my own and live life on my own terms. I had made some new friends and I was getting the hang of being a college student when I met him. He was one of the popular guys on campus.

Our story unfolded like one of the many romance novels I used to read in high school. He was tall with smooth dark skin and pretty white teeth. That was a lethal combination for me, my weakness personified. He was really big on working out, so his physique was like pow! Many of the girls on campus had their sights on him, but I pretended that I didn't notice him at all. He approached me one night at a house party. We talked for a while and he asked if he could take me out. I thought about him for the rest of the night in my dorm room. I kept thinking to myself, *"What does he see in me? He can have any girl that he wants."*

After our first date, we began spending everyday together. He was renting a house off campus with a roommate and he wanted me to stay at his house every night. There were nights when I wanted to stay in my dorm room, but he would persist until I agreed to stay with him. We had so many late night conversations about the future, about our feelings for each other. I fell head over heels in love with this man. We laughed together and we cried together. I truly believed that he would be my husband and my happily ever after.

I remember the day when I realized that I might be pregnant. We were at his house sitting on the sofa talking. I was laughing at something then I began to cough. In the midst of me coughing, I started to feel like I needed to throw up, so I ran to the bathroom. I made it just in time to throw up in the bathroom sink. He ran in behind me and asked if I was okay.

He gave me a towel to wipe my face and then he asked me, "Are you pregnant?" I shrugged it off and said no. After a couple of weeks, I did notice that my period was late. I mentioned it to him, and we bought a pregnancy test. The test was positive, and he was so happy about it. He called his mom the same day but not me! I was so afraid to tell my mom. I knew she would be disappointed in me. I was supposed to be in college getting my education, not out there getting pregnant. When I finally did tell her, the response was way better than I thought it would be. She was disappointed but also supportive.

As time went on and the pregnancy progressed, I started to notice a change in his attitude. I began to see some selfish ways in him. I think that reality set in and he realized he wasn't ready to put another life ahead of his own. We stopped having sex and I felt like he was not physically attracted to me anymore because of the weight gain from the baby. I still had a glimmer of hope that he would do something special for me on Valentine's Day.

The day came and went with no call or visit from him. I called him the next day to ask why I hadn't heard from him and that's when he broke it off. I cried uncontrollably for days after that. I felt betrayed. We had several conversations about having a baby before I got pregnant. He asked me to stop taking my birth control so that we could make a baby together.

I replayed every conversation that we had over and over in my head to make sure I didn't make up some fantasy but I knew that was not the case. I felt stupid but that experience matured me very quickly. That was my first lesson about reality.

Dear Single Mom,

Many of us did not choose the path of single motherhood. We all arrived here in different ways. I'm here to let you know that there is life abundantly for you even after becoming a single mother. Keep God first and you'll never feel like you're doing this alone.

Erica Warren is a best-selling author of Dear Young Woman. She is a passionate cheerleader for women who want to speak their truth and heal from their past.

Her motto is: "I will be the person that I needed when I was younger." Erica is a former customer service agent in the banking industry who is now an independent agent in the financial services industry.

She loves to educate the next generation about money and how to leave a legacy behind for their families. Erica was born and raised in Franklinton, LA and is now a current resident of Hammond LA. She is a proud mother of four sons ranging in ages from thirteen to twenty-three.

To learn more about this author, you can follow her on Instagram @e_class100, on Facebook @Author Erica Warren or you can catch an episode of her podcast called The Code of Sisterhood on Spotify, Google podcasts or Anchor.fm

2

The Trinity

I could barely get the words out of my mouth to ask the person on the other line to bring me a pregnancy test home. I mean, God forbid someone I knew saw me purchasing a pregnancy test for myself from the local pharmacy; if that wouldn't make inner city news at five, I don't know what would. Lucky for me, no questions were asked, and two tests were in my hands by the end of the night.

I sat in my bathroom reluctant to take the test but knew I could not put it off any longer. What was the big issue? Women were having babies without husbands since the beginning of time. My mother had me out of wedlock, and I like to think that I didn't turn out so bad. I giggled to myself as I remembered talking among my friends in high school boldly stating that I wanted to be a baby's mother. Silly me!

All I have seen at the time was the materialistic items; I was an outsider with no affiliation with the internal circle. I mean, the cheating was evident but the abuse—mentally, physically, emotionally, and psychologically—I was not privy to. I had no idea that those words I stated so confidently would mold my future. If I chose to keep this child growing inside of me, I would have gained access to an elite class: the single mother's society.

July 30, 2006, changed my life forever. I gave birth to a healthy baby girl through an emergency c-section. I did not know that the fairy tale life I had imagined with my child's father would turn into a true reality TV series for the books. I couldn't understand how I was cooped up in a hospital for almost seven days and this man I just gave a child to, could not stay for seven hours.

Once home, I received much help from my child's godmother (who was my roommate at the time), family, and close friends. I could not understand for the life of me, why my child's father was not as engaged as other people's baby's father. Until a piece of the puzzle was presented; there was someone else.

At first, it was a hard pill to swallow, since my daughter's father had been on my heels for years. He told anyone who would listen that I was the one he wanted, and he desired to spend the rest of his life with me. There was nothing he wouldn't do for me. I mean, in the beginning, he didn't even present his true self to me; then when he did, he told me that he only hid certain things because of the type of female I was, he didn't think he would have a chance. A little weird to me, but to others, they would try to convince me how sweet that was and an expression of how much he desired me.

One of my biggest problems was always letting people manipulate my thinking (good thing I didn't let that happen with my choice of going away to college). "Overlook his flaws because no one is perfect," and "Stop being so hard on him," are things that would constantly be said. So I took heed. I mean, I went to catholic school for twelve years and was taught to forgive others.

Two and a half years of a threesome drove me insane. Running up on the other woman; he and the other woman; it just got old. He finally decided that he wanted to be a family and left her alone (so I thought) and I had regained my rightful place in his life. Many people told me, "See girl, you just had to be patient and he would come around." The crazy thing is that didn't sit well with me. I remember having sex with him and thinking, "I don't even want to be with him anymore."

All those sleepless nights, students coming into my class reporting they saw my daughter's father in their housing project that morning, being laughed at, and talked about; I was playing myself. Something was birthed during intercourse that night: PAYBACK. After we were done, I told him it was over and for the next few years, I showed him better than I could tell him. I had no care for his feelings or what he tried to do to get back in my good graces. I allowed my mother to talk me into giving him another chance; played with the idea and exited left shortly after.

So, how in the world did I end up having another child ten years later—after vowing to be done only to end back up in the same threesome I thought I gained victory over? Listening to people who I thought had my best interest at heart. And let me be clear, they may have based things on their own exposure and experiences. Yes, I had another child by this man, and I thought this time was different. I went through some post-partum depression and because communication was not our strong suit, he found his way back to the old thing that had been there for him before.

I get it, because there was a point in time when he was the old thing that I fell back on because of the familiarity but the cycle had to stop. This threesome hit different; it took me out. I had no drive, no desire to win, and could not even get it together for the two people whose lives depended on me. I began to make very poor decisions, which I am mature enough to take responsibility for. I no longer wanted to be anyone's baby mother and look forward to being a wife to a worthy king. Boy, has the single mom's society taught me a thing or two.

Dear Single Mom,

Know that your words have power and shape your

tomorrow. When receiving advice, look at the fruit and know people's motives. True motives take time because everyone in your life does not want to see you win. Make sure you have a solid team that will throw a prayer up as well as keep it real no matter how hard it may be.

Paulette Bosley is a social butterfly who hails from Connecticut, holding a Bachelor of Art Degree in Elementary Education from the illustrious Tuskegee University.

She is a mother of two beautiful children; daughter: Dillyn, fourteen and son: Dash, four. Paulette enjoys traveling, spending time with family and close friends, dancing, and having a good time. She is the founder of Posh Dynasty, which is an empowerment group for young girls ages five to eighteen; and Fly Mommies, which is a support group for Mothers.

You can find her encouraging someone or teaching a dance class at HADM. Keep your eyes open, as she will be selling homes as a CT realtor.

3

Lessons from a Single Mom

From before I can remember, I've always looked forward to becoming a mother. As the oldest of eight children, I had the pleasure of watching my mom's motherhood journey. I noticed how patient she was with us even though I knew we were getting on her last nerve. Or how she sacrificed her last, whether it was food, money, etc., to make sure that our needs were met.

Despite the challenges of motherhood, my mom gracefully and lovingly cared for us. Her selflessness and patience were two traits that I admired and was determined to let be the basis of how I would one day parent. Fast forward to now. It's 2020 and I am now a mother and have been for two years. However, never did I anticipate that I would be a SINGLE MOTHER.

My dream of motherhood always included marriage first with "mini-me's" to follow. But here I am raising my son by myself with very little support from his father. Now, I'm aware of the decisions I've made that have brought me to this place in life and have made my peace with it, but that still doesn't make being a single mother any easier. Though I'm still new to my motherhood journey, I've learned so much in this short period of time; lessons that I pray will encourage you.

Lesson #1: You are not alone.

There were so many days that I'd cry just feeling the loneliness and the burden of raising a child alone. When my son's father was still in the picture, we would talk about everything: what to feed our son when he started eating solid food, how to deal with his eczema, plans for his future, etc. It was nice to have a sounding board and someone around to co-parent with. But when he abruptly left, it felt like the weight of the world was on my shoulder.

I felt like no one understood how I felt. I was overwhelmed. As I cried, I was reminded that God is always with me. Deuteronomy 31:6 became my go-to scripture whenever I was feeling alone and overwhelmed. *"Be strong and courageous, do not be afraid or tremble in dread before them, for it is the Lord your God who goes with you. He will not fail you or abandon you."*

Eventually, I ended up joining a mom's group with little ones that were around my son's age. We were able to share our challenges of being new parents, and for the first time in a long time, I felt seen. I felt understood. So when you are feeling alone and overwhelmed, FIRST call out to God. He will be your ever-present help whenever you need it. Then find a community of like-minded mommies that will provide you with much-needed advice and support.

Lesson #2: Lose the expectations.

Much like myself, I'm sure many of you dreamed about one day becoming a mother, fantasizing about the type of mother you would be, etc. Then you became a mother and everything you thought you'd do, you didn't do, and the things you said you'd never do, you did!! Hey, I even thought that because I was the oldest of eight and had "helped raise my siblings," being a parent would be a breeze. Boy was I wrong!!

I soon realized that I had all these expectations defining who I SHOULD be, but not representing who I really AM. How many of you have felt this way or still feel this way? Who said I had to be a certain type of mom? Society? Family? Friends? Too many of us have let everyone else define what it means to be a mother.

According to the Merriam-Webster dictionary, a mother is defined as "a female parent." Plain and simple. That definition is very broad, which means YOUR definition of a "mother" lies within YOU. At the end of the day, you are still an individual with your own thoughts, ideas, and a plethora of life experiences to draw from.

No one woman is going to parent the same as another. Embrace your uniqueness. Don't let another person's expectations box you into a corner or make you question who you are. Don't even let your own preconceived fantasies define you. I'm also sure you didn't expect to be a single mother, but don't even let "being a single mom" keep you from being your best self. As a dear friend often reminds me, "Your journey is your own."

Lesson #3: Let God be your guide as you parent your child(ren).

One day, I was working on client work and my son was playing with some of his toys. I looked down just to see what he was doing and saw that he had found some styrofoam and was breaking it up on the floor. Immediately, I told him to "stop making a mess" (something my parents would have definitely said). However, the Holy Spirit stopped me mid-sentence and told me to let him play with it.

At first, I was a little frustrated because I knew I'd be the one to have to clean up the mess... But the Holy Spirit showed me, 1) he needs to explore and learn what different textures and things feel like... He was only 16 months old. This is how he learns. And 2) the Holy Spirit said, "No, you won't have to clean up the mess, you will teach him how to."

I let him play with the styrofoam (of course, making sure he didn't put any in his mouth). When he was finished and was ready to move to the next thing, I stopped him and told him that we were going to clean up the mess he made first. I got the vacuum cleaner (I let him walk down the hall with me and bring it back to the room), pulled out the attachment, and TAUGHT him how to clean up the mess he made.

At that moment, God showed me that if I allowed Him, He would show me how to parent my son. God reminded me that he created my son and knows exactly what lessons he needs to learn to become the man He's called him to be. Sometimes you may feel nervous about parenting, be at a loss for what to do, or just resort back to raising your child(ren) the way you were raised. However, take a moment and commit parenting your child(ren) to the Lord. He will lead and guide you to show you exactly what to do.

Dear Single Mom,

You are not alone. Don't be defined by others' expectations of what a mother should look like. And if you let God, He will show you exactly how to be the woman and mother He's called you to be!

Stephanie Lee, a native of Atlanta, Georgia, is a single mom, an entrepreneur, and a first-time author. She is the owner/CEO of The ROSE Brand, a branding, design, and event management firm.

Inspired by her role as a new mom, Stephanie recently created I Am A Mom Boss, a blog and online community for "mompreneurs." "As a new mom, I've experienced so many challenges with juggling the responsibilities of being a mother and business owner. I wanted to create a safe space for women mastering both motherhood and the boardroom." In her leisure time, Stephanie enjoys spending time with her two-year-old son.

You can connect with Stephanie on Facebook or Instagram at @therosebrand / @iamamomboss
Visit her websites: www.therosebrand.com or www.iamamomboss.com.

4

God will Give You Beauty for Ashes

For as long as I can remember, I wanted to be a mother. I envisioned myself having two or three kids, and I used to wonder what it would sound like for someone to call me mom. I met the one that I thought I would spend the rest of my life with, in college. When he graduated, I still had two and a half years remaining in school. I was so "in-love" with him, that I ended up getting engaged, leaving school, and moving to his state. Two days after we got married, I found out that I was pregnant.

I brought a healthy baby girl into this world, with just my husband and his mom by my side. Looking back at it, I never realized how much I needed my own mom in that moment, but she was way across the country in the home that I left. After my daughter was born, things started to change in my marriage. As I focused on being a good mom and doing everything that I thought I was supposed to be doing, I was told by my husband, that I was giving my daughter more attention than I was giving him.

I had to figure out how to balance being a new wife and a new mother all in less than a year, in addition to being in a new state where I didn't have any family or friends. Seventeen months after I had my daughter, I had another baby that came as a surprise. By the time my son was born, my marriage was hanging on by a thread. My husband was staying out late at night, he started having angry outburst towards me, and was drinking very heavily. I really wanted out of my marriage, but I was too ashamed and embarrassed to tell my family what I was going through because I went against everybody's opinions of my moving.

Feelings of being a single mother came long before I was even officially a single mother. I was lonely and felt like no one understood what I was going through. When my son was born, my husband was passed out drunk in the delivery room, and the only ones who were there to support me was God, and the anesthesiologist, while I was having a cesarean section. Both of my babies were in diapers at the same time when my marriage became abusive emotionally, physically, and psychologically. One of the worst moments in that period of time, was when I came home one night and found my newborn son laying on the living room floor screaming because he had fallen off the couch.

My husband was passed out drunk on the floor next to him. My daughter was asleep in her crib in the bedroom. Of course, I went off on a tangent, and we started arguing. My husband grabbed a knife and gave me the impression that he was going to stab me with it. Right then, I knew that if God did not get me out of the situation, no one could. Eventually, after a few more traumatizing events with my husband, I finally decided to choose the peace of mind, and safety of my children and myself, and I left my marriage.

When my son was about two years old, it was determined that he could not hear, and he was also later on diagnosed with having autism. I had to learn how to help him communicate effectively by myself, and while he had to attend special education and speech therapy classes, I battled with wondering what I did wrong as to why my child had to endure this challenge.

I finally obtained my bachelor's degree when my kids were in middle school, and over the years, I have struggled financially to care for my children with minimal help from my ex-husband. I had gotten a court order for child support in my divorce decree, but raising two active kids with only the bare minimum, it was a constant struggle. I have worked two jobs, been on food stamps, hustled, and even felt like I sold my soul to the devil on a few occasions, for the sake of making sure my children had what they needed financially.

I became bitter when my ex-husband was off living his best life while I was struggling to take care of our kids without his help. There were many nights that I cried when he would refuse to give me a break and come get them and spend time with them. Eventually, God placed people in my life who became my angels and would help with my kids so I could rejuvenate and restore.

Both of my children decided to go to college in two different states three to five hours from where we live. Every semester, I have had to figure out how we would come up with the money to pay their part of the tuition that financial aid did not cover. My ex-husband told us in so many words, that we were on our own with paying for school. However, he'd send money here and there for groceries or miscellaneous things. Nevertheless, God has always provided a way for their tuitions to be paid, and with His help, my daughter graduated from college in May 2020, and my son will be graduating in May 2021.

Dear Single Mom,

I wish someone would have told me to trust God to provide for me and my children in every area of our lives. I wish I would have known to lean and depend on God only, and not put my trust in anybody else, but Him. I believe it would have saved me a lot of unnecessary heart-ache and headache. Regardless of what you go through, God is always with you, and everything that you go through is for a reason. However, in the end, God will always give you beauty for ashes. (Isaiah 61:3)

Antoinette (Toni) Davenport attended Grambling State University for four years and completed her Bachelor of Science in Psychology with a concentration in Criminal Justice through Argosy University.

She works for the State of Georgia and enjoys helping at-risk individuals get their lives back on track. Also, while living in Georgia, she has raised her two young adults.

Toni's strong faith in God allows her to believe that without His help, she would not make it through the hard times. One of her purposes, is to inspire other single moms to help them understand that they can also survive the times where they feel overwhelmed, insecure, and hopeless.

Toni can be contacted by email at prettytoni2000@yahoo.com and Facebook at www.facebook.com/toni.greendavenport.

5

Know Your Worth

I wanted to write about knowing your worth; yes, I said it! We must love ourselves and believe it no matter what. Not going on what others say or do, nor the negative narrative we tell ourselves. I know this topic is tough for some of us to deal with so let me start by telling you some of my story.

When I was younger, I always felt like nothing good was coming my way, not my father's love, nor even having things that everyone else seemed to have. So I always felt like I wasn't enough and that it was my fault that no one wanted to be around me. As a child of divorce or a broken family unit, I always felt like if I could have loved my dad more he would have stayed. Yet, as the years went by, he would pop up every now and then leaving my emotions and feelings in disarray. I always did anything I could to make him happy, hoping that he would show me that he loved me.

Nothing ever seemed to be enough, so I looked to other sources to fill the void. I looked to my friends to help bring the joy back into my life, but always seemed to come up lacking. I felt my world keep getting smaller and smaller, so, eventually, I just gave up on life in general. I was sixteen when I first attempted suicide, I took a bunch of pills and just hoped I wouldn't wake up.

I became so despondent that it didn't work that I decided to just go out and do anything I could to find love, I was living recklessly, drinking, and having sex with random people. I lied to people, about my name, and my age just so that I could feel loved. I was out of control doing things that were hard and could hurt more than heal. Then I had an encounter that would change my life forever. I was at church with one of my friends at a women's bible study on the book of Ruth. This older lady said something that really resonated with me, when Naomi told Ruth to go back to her home and to her people she refused. Ruth told her, "Wherever you go I go, and where

you stay, I stay, your people would be my people, and your God my God."

In that moment, I heard the Holy Spirit speaking to me like never before, he said, "Let God be your God, not the things others can or will give to you." In that moment, I realized that I had to be a better person and to not give up on myself. You see, there is a lot more to my story, but I just wanted to give you a small snippet of some of the things that I have struggled with. Now I'm a single mom raising a son in this ever-changing world that has shown me that nothing is freely given or easy, that you have to work hard at everything you do to succeed. I'm not saying that there is not a light at the end of the tunnel as the saying goes, but take heart, there is something better for us out there. When we seek out a relationship that is founded with the ultimate demonstration of love, everything can and will change.

There is a verse, John 16:33 Amplified version "I have told you these things, so that in Me you may have [perfect] peace and confidence. In the world you have tribulation and trials and distress and frustration; but be of good cheer [take courage, be confident, certain, undaunted]! For I have overcome the world. [I have deprived it of the power to harm you and conquered it for you.]" This verse has given me life and brought me back to my joy. Remember how we started off and I told you about how we have to love ourselves and change the negative narrative we tell ourselves?

Listening to the negative can cause a ripple effect that could last a lifetime, mine did and now I take my steps one at a time to get back to where I need to be. Well, you may say that's still overwhelming. Can I offer you the source that for me has helped make my way easier? Having a relationship with God was the one thing that kept me moving on many days. I get frustrated and angry, I get worried and fearful, I get anxious and full of sorrow, but God is still there. No matter what we have done or felt about ourselves or how we treat and are treated by others, God is still there for us.

Dear Single Mom,

You are never alone. There is an army of woman around you from every walk of life who has been in the same position you have been. Whether it's having this child or children on your own, to having a past that you are not proud of, don't fret; it's all helped to make you who you are. Let the lessons you have learned in life be the words that you share with the next woman who comes along and needs a word to lift her up. Your past sorrow could be the branch that can help another woman find her voice and skip over some trauma that may have been in their path.

Your outreach of love can help heal a deep wound that may be festering and ready to blow the fractured pieces of her heart into the nether. I just wanted to encourage you and let you know you are loved, cherished, and valued. How can I know? Remember, there is more than you know to everyone's story, that shapes and molds them into good or bad; it makes us who we are. You got this, and I believe in you!

Jes Willis is a single mother from Virginia. When she isn't writing, she is running around with her son and her three fur babies, her dogs. Her other interests are creating beautiful one of a kind jewelry and mastering her painting and drawing skills.

She is also very involved with a mentoring and discipleship program that helps single moms and families coping with grief and loss, empowering them to take back control of their situations.

6

It Will Get Better

I remember so vividly the moment that I found out I was expecting my son. I had so many thoughts and emotions running through my mind. I was scared, felt alone, and even contemplated on having an abortion. Why? Well, because I was working a job making minimum wage, riding in a small two-door car, and my son's father was not the most dependable person financially.

I did not want to have a child under those circumstances. I had a college degree, but no success finding a career in my field of study. I was not prepared to be anyone's mother. Well, at least, that was what I thought. When I was about five months pregnant, I kept going back and forth as to whether I wanted to apply for the WIC Program for government assistance because I was a very private person and did not want people to even know that I was expecting at the time.

Finally, I scheduled the appointment. The day of the appointment will always be memorable to me. During the application process, the WIC Clerk asked about my employment and the hourly rate. I was so embarrassed to tell her that I was working at Walgreens as a Service Clerk making $7.25 per hour. When she asked about my educational background, I was excited to tell her that I had graduated from Delta State University with a bachelor's degree in Nutrition and Business Administration. She then stated, "We need you here!" She went on to say that they did not have a permanent Nutritionist at the clinic and was looking to hire one.

The supervisor contacted me a few days later to set up an appointment for an interview. I had a trip planned to go to Florida for my niece's graduation, so I asked if we could schedule the interview around my trip because I had already bought a plane ticket. The supervisor agreed to meet me at a restaurant in Jackson before boarding the plane. I received a phone call from the supervisor while I was on vacation that I had the job. That was music to my ears! My prayers had been answered. I finally had a career as a Nutritionist and could provide for my son without depending on anyone.

September 27th, my son was born. After I laid eyes on him, I thanked God that I did not go through with the abortion. On the same day I delivered him, I had just started classes for my master's degree. The professor asked me if I needed to sit out for a while due to having my son. That was not an option for me. I knew I had to do whatever I needed to do in order to be successful and financially stable.

On September 20, 2013, I resigned from my first career because I was eager to be even more successful after having my son. I did not want to raise my son in MS. I moved to Tampa, FL with no plan at all, sleeping on an air bed in a family member's house, getting food stamps, and looking for a job for months without any success. I was draining my savings and felt like I was back at step one. As a single mother, I always feel like I have to over overcompensate so that my son does not feel like he is missing out on anything. As I predicted, my son's father was not the most dependable financially.

He was sending money whenever he decided to send money, so I had to turn to child support. It was a relief not having to call and ask him for money and not knowing whether I would receive the money or not. I used to depend on my son for my happiness. I remember the first summer he went to stay with his dad. I had never been away from him for such a long period of time. I did not know how to live without him. Everything I did revolved around him. The separation anxiety was so bad that I had to turn to antidepressants and therapy to cope with him being gone. I used to worry about him so much that I could not function. But God!! I learned to start living again and I stopped feeling like I always had to be in mommy mode. I am no longer dependent on antidepressants!!

I will never forget the morning that I was driving and listening to Steve Harvey's Morning Show. Steve said, "How do you expect God to get you where you want to go if you are not giving him something to put his finger on?" I had given up because I was not getting call backs from jobs that I knew I qualified for. That evening, I completed application after application and finally got a call from the State of Florida for an interview.

The day of the interview arrived! At the end of the interview, the lady told me that they were going to select someone that was already an employee because they like to promote from within. She then stated, but I have another position that you could apply for and we can set up an interview tomorrow. I went to the interview the next day and was hired!! My career has been elevating since that day.

It took me a while to get where I am today, but I have a career with the State of Florida as an inspector for Nursing Homes in seven different counties. I am also the CEO/founder of LG Financial Services.

Dear Single Mom,

Continue to work hard for whatever it is that you want. It may not come when you want it, but I promise it will eventually happen if you apply yourself and trust God. Continue to pursue your dreams and be the best mother that you can be. You have a little one depending on you!

Latoya Gordon is a single mom to one, career woman, entrepreneur, and author. She currently resides in Tampa, FL. Latoya received a Bachelor of Nutrition and Business Administration at Delta State University and a Master of Public Health at Grand Canyon University.

She is currently employed by the State of Florida as an inspector for nursing homes. Latoya is the CEO of LG Financial Services providing tax preparation, notary, and credit repair services. Her goal is to say goodbye to the guilt of being a single mom and to continue filling the void of the missing piece in her son's life.

To connect with her, send an email to latoya@lgfinancialservicesonline.com. Follow her on Facebook at www.facebook.com/LatoyaGordon and on Instagram at www.instagram.com/latoyavgordon.

7

"Worthy Love"

If I were to ask you to truly examine your thoughts and your desire to be loved completely, I wonder what your response would be. I wonder, to what extent would you go to find the love that you so badly desire? I am not necessarily speaking of just romantic love, but just the idea of constantly feeling the need to receive outside affirmation and validation. Honestly, it's like a drug, it can be very addictive and very dangerous all at the same time. You begin to look for love in all the wrong places. Not caring what the side effects may be, but anything to have that instant gratification. And before you realize it, you're in a cycle.

A cycle that just keeps going and going and going. You catch my drift. And as the time passes, pieces of you are slowly stripped away. So much to the point that you don't even recognize yourself any longer. But little did you know, the love that you had been searching for was within you the whole while.

If I had realized the value of what "that touch" would cost me for many years of my life, I probably would have talked with someone about it. You may ask, what touch are you referring to? Well, it was the touch of a family friend and the words that came with it, asking me, "Do you want to know what it feels like to be kissed down there?" And, of course, at such a young age, I had no clue what that meant, so I said yes.

I didn't realize that her being in those intimate places was totally inappropriate and just flat out wrong. From this point—yep, you guessed it—my innocence was out the door. Because now that I thought that this was normal behavior, I wanted to experience that feeling again and again. It was something that I never felt that I could address, and I wasn't quite sure how It would be received.

So, for years of my life, I had relationships that ranged from, on and off again, relationships that were just no good for me. Guys that were unavailable all together, whether it was mentally, emotionally, or if they were with someone else, that didn't matter. All In hopes to have the attention and affection that I had so badly desired. I believed and accepted half trues, which we know were just flat out lies. I didn't value myself and absolutely didn't value the scaredness of sex. I knew how to dress the part, how to keep myself extremely busy, and how to always deflect the attention off my true issues. Which were, low self-esteem, I didn't know my identity, nor my self-worth.

By age twenty-five, I was still unmarried, and I didn't have any kids. That year, I was introduced to my then husband and nine months later, we were married. Yep, you read that correctly. It would take me a great length of time to elaborate all that had unfolded within this time. But in short, within a year of being married, things fell apart. And I was back home with my family, facing divorce, and then became a single mother.

Every aspect of this situation was complicated. The amount of guilt and shame that was experienced, I would not wish it on anyone. I felt as though I had let God, my family, and myself down. Sometimes I reflect on where I was mentally and it's all a blur. There were times I had to pull strength that I didn't even realize that I had, to be present for my child. In this season of my life, I truly began to experience God as my keeper.

I began to realize that I had to get to the root of the problem and the true issues. The truth was, I didn't completely understand my identity in Christ. There were times when all I could do was just cry out and pray specifically for God to keep my mind. Sometimes that was all that I had the strength to say.

As the days turned into weeks and weeks turned into months, I was finally able to get a hold of the postpartum depression and bouts of anxiety that I had been experiencing. I began to get into a routine that would help me. I would go to the gym because I knew that it would temporarily shift my thinking and it was also a way to reduce any anxiety. I would oftentimes go to the public library to use the resources there to read to my son, to journal, and look up scriptures to guide me.

I gathered learning videos and I also used it as an escape from my reality. If I could be honest, I truly believe that throughout this whole process, God was using my

son to display His unconditional love for me. I say this because the fact that I wanted to be the best mother that I could possibly be to my child, challenged me to look inward.

As the years passed, I could slowly feel my confidence rising. I can't say that I was the Miracle that I had known previously, but what I can say is, God used this entire experience to begin to strip away some very unhealthy cycles. I would describe it as me being gracefully broken. It was a very tough process, but It was done in such a way that only He can get the glory for it. He began to show me my identity in Him.

Dear Single Mom,

If I could leave you with any words of encouragement, I would tell you, you have been Graced for this. No, the situation may not be ideal. Yes, it is very challenging, trust me I know. But one thing that I do know is that God will see you through. Trust the process and trust that He is keeping you.

Miracle Turner Peters, is a native of Covington, LA. She is the mother of onc son. Her passions include encouraging women to truly understand their worth and God-given identity. She desires to take her past struggles and mistakes to encourage others that they are worthy of love.

She knows that if it had not been for her relationship with Christ, she would not be able to identify with what the true definition of either is, her God-given identity and love. She will continue to be rooted in the love of Christ and share that love with all who she crosses paths with. In the future, she desires to continue to do motivational speaking and writing.

8

Embracing Your Journey

Embrace: To accept or support (a belief, theory, or change) willingly and enthusiastically.

Journey: An act of traveling from one place to another; a voyage.

Have you ever thought about how your life was going to turn out? I am talking about having your life all planned out. I thought I did, until life happened.

One fall night, a friend and I went to see Samuelle perform his hit single, "So You Like What You See" at Club Broadway in Sauget, IL. I bumped into a tall, dark, and handsome man. He introduced himself and from that moment we talked and danced for the rest of the night. The beginning of our relationship started.

After a few years of dating, I found out I was pregnant with my first daughter. I never thought I would be a single parent, but there I was. For the next four years of dating off and on, we got married. I gained an amazing bonus son, and we had another daughter, completing our family. A couple of weeks after our second anniversary, our marriage was over, and the nastiness of divorce began along with being a single parent…again. This time it was different. I was really on my own now.

When my youngest daughter turned two years old, a major setback happened which turned our lives upside down and life as we knew it changed forever. After receiving the MMR vaccine, her life skills started to gradually regress until they were gone. After years of tests, she was officially diagnosed with Autism when she turned five years old. A few years later, she was diagnosed with Scoliosis, years later came Rheumatoid Arthritis, and a few years later TMJ deterioration. She became nonverbal, non-ambulatory and totally dependent. Raising a child with special needs is incredibly challenging but it is extremely rewarding at the same time.

My daughter went through different phases with each phase being worse than the one before. I had no clue when or where the meltdowns would happen. I did not know if I would ignore, cry, cuss a person out or beat them down if they looked at my daughter the wrong way or said the wrong thing. My emotions were all over the place. She went from constantly clapping her hands which created blisters, from running to walking from walking to crawling from crawling to nothing.

Sleepless nights from seizures and muscle spasms was one of the worst phases we experienced, but what impacted her more than anything, happened on Friday, 1 July 2016. Her left femur was fractured, during her doctor's visit, and required surgery. The healing process lasted ten weeks rather than the initial six weeks. By that time, her body had become severely contracted. The impact from that fracture is still being felt today.

Having to fight to get the correct medical and educational diagnosis/plans/support services, going to therapy sessions, getting my oldest daughter through elementary school and college, attending her extra-curricular activities while having a full-time job can take its toll. After a while,

I started to resent everybody and everything. This included family, friends, strangers, even God. I was mad at the world! I resented Homecoming/Prom/Graduation seasons. I did not want to hear about what parents were doing with their children.

I resented God for making my child that way so much that I would scream, "Why is my child in so much freaking pain? Why did my child lose her life skills? What did I do to make you punish her?" Being resentful was not making the situation any better, so I knew I had to deal with the hand I was dealt. One night, I went to kiss my daughter goodnight. She looked at me as if she were saying that she was sorry for being the way she was. She sensed all the negative energy I had. That broke my heart.

I come from a close-knit family and they have always had my back, but my rocks were my mother and sister. They cried with me, prayed with and for me, and encouraged me especially when I would breakdown. When my mother transitioned, we were devastated. Everything changed. The only thing I can say about that time is, depression is real!

Fast forward one year, I turned everything off and started talking to God, saying, "I know you are God all by yourself, I know you don't need my help, but please tell me what I need to do to help my baby. She is in so much pain, I am her protector, but I feel so helpless. Please quiet everything around me so I can hear from you."

I heard that still small voice, but of course I ignored it. One month later, God knocked me down and told me, "It's time for you to trust Me." That night was the start of our new beginning. God started placing people in my life that has caused me to unlearn things I was taught and relearn them the right way, from spirituality to health/wellness to wealth. Your mindset must change to move forward.

As a child, I prayed for patience, courage and understanding. I now know it was because God was preparing me for this journey. It is said that in life we have choices. I did not choose this journey, but I chose to embrace it. Through all the trials and triumphs, I am honored and grateful that God chose me to be the mother to go on this journey with them. As parents, we are supposed to teach our children, but my daughters have taught me more about life and myself than they know. I am who I am because of them!

Dear Single Mom,

Embrace who you are and your divine purpose. God specifically placed you on your personal journey and has equipped you with everything you need. You have been assigned this mountain to show others it can be moved. Keep moving forward. The best is yet to come!

Lillious Lumpkins is a single mother of two daughters, with her youngest having special needs. She is an author, "Cashflow Strategist," and co-owner of 5Factor Consulting LLP where we offer credit services, proven wealth building strategies including tax minimization, debt elimination, increasing cashflow, creating investment income, discount travel memberships, and more.

Lillious is the youngest of seven children, residing in St. Louis, Missouri. Fun fact: Lillious' fifty-second birthday turned out to be a historic day in St. Louis. The St. Louis Blues won the Stanley Cup for the first time in fifty-two years.

Contact information:
Email: info@5factorconsulting.com
Website: www.5factorconsulting.com
www.lilliouslumpkins.com
Facebook: https://www.facebook.com/lillious.lumpkins

LinkedIn: https://www.linkedin.com/in/lillious-lumpkins-89129253

Instagram: https://www.instagram.com/lillious007

9

Beauty for Ashes

As I sat there staring at the list of outstanding bills and a bank account balance of negative $500, I could not see how things would get better. I was already working two jobs as a registered nurse and applying to as many nurse practitioner positions as I could. The hospitals I was employed at were putting the staff on call or canceling our shifts and all I could do was pray. My daily prayer would consistently say, “Please God, just allow me to be able to feed my children.” Because that prayer would be answered without delay, I found peace in my situation while trying to hold on to my faith truly the size of a mustard seed.

At this point, all I could do was try my hardest not to be tempted to call any ex or old flames. I would call them flames to remind myself that going back would only burn me. Opening up sexually to them would guarantee that my negative bank account balance, past due bills, and even a little gift or two would be taken care of. This was hard to ignore because next to my list of bills sat a notice from my apartment complex to proceed with the eviction process.

However, I could not forget about my yes to God. So, I pushed the thoughts of the past aside and settled in my spirit that I trusted God. If I were evicted, I came up with a quick plan. My daughter would possibly go by her grandmother and my son would go by his dad. I would put my belongings in storage and keep a praise on my tongue, even through tears of uncertainty.

A little over five months prior to this, I thought I had it all. I created this life that pleased me and made me happy. Until it all came crashing down in the form of a horrible break-up, my new job falling through, and friendships ending. I found myself on the bathroom floor at 3 a.m. crying and I heard clearly, "I DO NOT SUBMIT TO YOU, YOU SUBMIT TO MY WILL FOR YOUR LIFE."

The days following, I gave God my yes. My yes to Him meant so much more than just being holy or the appearance there of. It meant accepting the life He has for me. I reminded myself constantly that to experience something new I had to do something new, give him my ashes.

Those ashes were giving up my old ways of manipulation through sex, healing from everything I allowed the world to deposit in me. Those ashes included the little girl who use to think about dying when she was supposed to be living. They included the teenager that was molested and when the fear of rape made her open her mouth, she was questioned, and no one believed her. The ashes contained the scared, confused twenty-year-old that was pregnant and tasted her blood more times than she would like to count. The ashes included the punches, beatings, pain from my mistakes. As I gave up the ashes, I began to allow God to heal me from the inside out.

Now, I am here, sitting at my table, not being able to see the future, and through my tears I heard, "FEED THE HOMELESS." I remember asking the Holy Spirit, "Feed the homeless?!? We are about to be the homeless!"

However, I got with my friends through a ministry we were trying to get going, With Open Arms Ministry, and we did just that. In November of 2017, I cooked sausage jambalaya, green beans, and peach cobbler. We handed out several Bibles with words of encouragement, gave hats, gloves, small blankets to several people. But that day, we left with so much more that we carry with us still. That evening, my kids ate the leftovers from that meal too.

Slowly, I accepted the fact that maybe it is not the time to work as a nurse practitioner. I remember before going to bed one night I spoke from a place of peace and reminded myself that I would continue praising God regardless. I started working more and was finally able to start catching up with my bills. I started being able to breathe and my faith continued to grow. Things were still tight, but at least there was no more eviction notices. A few days later, I was driving into a fast-food restaurant and got a phone call. It was the owner of a clinic I applied to a few weeks prior, and he said how impressed he was by my resume and would be honored to interview me.

I accepted my new job that day, even though I did not tell him by email until a few days later. Nevertheless, I knew while celebrating the New Year that I had a new experience waiting for me in 2018. That January, I started working as a Family Nurse Practitioner. I was so proud of where I was and humbled by the patients daily. Then in March, I received another phone call.

A few years prior, I wanted to purchase a home, but my financial situation and credit score did not make it a realistic option during that time. I put away that dream because I didn't think that would be an option until much later. The woman at the mortgage company told me that I must have been really working hard, because I was now pre-approved. I prayed about my decision and in June of 2018—exactly one year from when I whispered yes to God—I closed on my first home. Not just any home but, a five-bedroom/four-bathroom house with a pool and jacuzzi. I left from the title company and picked up my brand new 2018 BMW as well. Every day and every situation following, God has always remained faithful.

Dear Single Mom,

I understand about being in difficult seasons that seem as though it will never end. I understand the pain of living through your mistakes. You try to be the strongest person in the world but feel like the weakest. I can only imagine how many times you fell asleep in your own tears.

But know, I mean really KNOW, just how much you are loved by the greatest God of them all. That love is your strength. That love is for you continually and that love is what will allow you to keep holding on. Please let my story encourage you to know that this is all a part of God's plan. I am rooting for you. God is going to get the glory! Hold on my sister, because God is going to give you BEAUTY FOR ASHES.

From the small town of Sunset, Louisiana, **Aniece Nicole** currently resides in New Orleans with her two beautiful children, Tylan (fourteen) and Tyler (five). She is a family nurse practitioner, author, and co-founder of The Gift of Healing Hearts Ministry. Through the many storms of life, she has gained a true understanding of the love and faithfulness of God.

Her desire is to be an example that just as He delivered her, He will do the same for each one of his precious daughters. You may reach her on social media's platforms of IG: a_ni_kole14 and FB: Nicole Smith.

10

Learn to Live....

After my divorce, I became a single mother of two children. When I became a single mom, I was so afraid. I didn't really quite know where to begin. I had no money saved. I could not even purchase a gallon of milk. It was then that I knew I had to do something. This is where my journey began…

I took a job as a housekeeper for a local nursing home. I worked there to pay off my vehicle that I had at the time and to do my best to provide for my children and put food on the table. The job only paid $8.50 per hour. I know, right…How was I going to make it off that. I am educated, have a degree as a Computer Information Specialist, yet I could not find a job that paid a decent wage.

Every dime I made went towards my children and the household. I was on "Public Aid"—welfare is what most would call it. And child support was not that much. I was utilizing whatever assistance was available just to get by. I prayed and I prayed for God to continue to bless me to be able to provide for my babies. I was a single mom… I was not the first and I was not going to be the last. I had to learn to live.

Giving up was clearly not an option, I had two children watching me. An exceptionally good friend of mine gave me this concept: "You and your kids are a family; you all are a team. When one does not do their part you all fail." That resonated within me. I would have numerous conversations with my children explaining that we are a team, and we all had a part to do.

What I told them was I expected their absolute best because I give them my Absolute Best! There was no right or wrong way to do it. Life does not come with a manual. Every day we learn something new. For me, that was being the best mother I could be. No matter the obstacles that came my way, I had to Learn to Live.

I worked first shift jobs while my kids were in school during the day. I did not work nights as I wanted to be home at night with them. And I did not trust too many people. The trials came and many were so difficult. Many times, I wondered how I would even get through the day…I cried myself to sleep many nights praying and asking God for a way out! Man, was that tunnel dark. My kids would go visit with their father and depression would overtake me. I felt like the walls would be closing in. I would pray, cry, and scream. I would lay on my face before God. My shoulders were heavy, I did not want to fail as a mother. It gets difficult, it gets overwhelming. But I work extremely hard to ensure we would all be okay.

I teach my children about God and how to pray, we show love, we laugh, we sing we cry. My team…we are all we got. I give God all the glory as he leads and guides me every day. I hold on to my faith as it has taken me so far. God continues to see me through it all. I had to learn to live and so I did. I became resourceful, I became an entrepreneur. I couldn't find the job I wanted so I created jobs.

I'm not where I want to be just yet but by God's grace, one day, I will surely arrive. So glad I don't look like what I have been through. This journey has shaped me into who I am today. Life will knock you down, but you can always get up. As a mother, we wear many hats and guess what, we wear them well.

I began to hear people say, "Crisonda, you are such a good mom, your kids are so well mannered and respectful," and that made me feel so good inside. Even when I felt as though I failed, my children show me daily that I haven't. Learn to live, that's what I keep telling myself. I set goal and I achieve them all. As a single mom, I had to learn to live. And TODAY I'M DOING JUST THAT!!

Dear Single Mom,

I want to say you are amazing. No matter what it looks like, keep trusting God, keep going, keep striving. Your children are seeds that grow. We water them every day in how we treat them, how we talk to them, and how we love them. Giving them our absolute best. You will reap a great harvest. Deposit great things within your children and you will see the greatness that will come from them. Have no regrets. Embrace the journey that you lead for your children to see just how great you are!

Philippians 1:6 – "For I am confident in this one thing, He who began a good work in you will perfect it until the day of Christ Jesus."

God Bless

Crisonda Watson, a thirty-nine-year-old mother of two, a serial entrepreneur with a strong zeal to write. She is a co-author in a collaborative publication entitled "In Spite Of It All" (stories compiled by Erica Warren).

She holds an associate's degree as a Computer Information Specialist as well as a Diploma for Personal Business for Computers. Also, she has three businesses registered in Illinois. Currently working as the Director of her own employment agency, Starrtemps Staffing. She also has a networking platform called, "Blackronicles." and a former family childcare business called "Starr Child Daycare." On her latest project, she is a podcast host for her relationship platform called "The Treasure Box."

She was born and raised in Erie, PA and currently resides in Joliet, IL. She is an amazing mother to her loving son, Joshua, and her loving daughter, Cianna.

Being a single mom, she has faced many challenges and now knows that life will teach you many things.

She has always loved writing and wants to inspire others to be the best version of themselves in whatever they do in life. Always remember, "Nothing beats a trial but a failure." If you don't try, you will never know the potential you have inside.

Follow me on Instagram @CandiKane81
Facebook page @Crisonda Watson

11

Not Defined by My Singleness

Single Mom - I Am, Limited by My Singleness – I Am Not. As single moms, we are not limited or less than because of our singleness. If anything, we are stronger because of it. We are stronger because we are educated. We are stronger because we are gainfully employed. We are stronger because we are business owners. We are stronger because we are leaders. We are stronger because we are motivators. We are stronger because we are the heads of our households. We are stronger because we are all of these amazing things in the midst of, often times, having little or no support.

I became a mom at the age of twenty-three while in my last semester of college (or what I thought would be my last semester). I had experienced a few setbacks while in college and was beyond ready to graduate, only to discover that I was expecting! In spite of my unplanned pregnancy, I was determined to graduate on time but then the unexpected happened! My daughter made her arrival into this world three and a half months early! I was due to have her in late October and she arrived mid-June halting my plans to graduate that semester, especially considering that she was born in a completely different state, six hours away from home.

Going into labor prematurely while vacationing was an experience of a lifetime! We had to remain in the state of Florida for three months until she was healthy enough to go home. The experience of having a baby three and a half months early and temporarily relocating to another state with no family and friends, made me realize that I was a lot stronger and braver than I ever knew.

After being away for three months, we were finally able to return home and I now had to figure out a plan to care for my newborn baby, who because of her premature birth could not attend daycare, and re-enroll in school. Her father lived in another state, three hours away from us, and while I had the support of my parents, she was my responsibility to care for. I sat out of school for an additional semester and returned in spring of the following year to earn my first college degree.

My daughter became my biggest motivation. Providing her with the best life possible and raising her to be a respectful, loving, ambitious girl who would come to recognize her value and worth as a young lady rested solely on my shoulders. I could not fail her, and I didn't want her to experience some of the unnecessary hardships in life that I had experienced. She had to be better than me so I worked extra hard on myself and at being successful so that she could have every opportunity to do so. When she was six years old, I decided to go back to school to get a Master of Business Administration degree.

With a full-time job and being a full-time mom, I knew this would be challenging but I also knew that obtaining this degree would take my career to the next level, allowing me to better provide for my daughter, so despite the difficulty that lied ahead I re-enrolled in school anyway! There were many late nights of studying after I put her to bed; some nights I didn't sleep at all and went right to work the next morning. My weekends were often consumed with studying which sometimes meant less time with my daughter.

Although she was only six, I often explained to her that my being in school would provide a better life for us and I have to say, I often found myself apologizing to her for having to study so much and not be as present. Nevertheless, "we" got through it and she witnessed her mom working extra hard to accomplish something that appeared to be quite challenging. I believe this experience allowed her to know that she too will be able to accomplish great things in the face of adversity.

Often times, we try to hide our struggles from our children, but I believe it's good to allow them to see us struggle a little and witness us overcoming, so that they can know that when life presents them with obstacles, they too can overcome. I want my daughter to know that life can be overwhelming and challenging at times but more importantly, I want her to know that she is strong and capable of accomplishing amazing things. Just as I want my daughter to know this, I want the same for you.

Dear Single Mom,

You are not defined by your singleness. Being a single mom who bears the responsibility of raising your children on your own makes you so strong and you should be very proud of yourself. It's often easier to accomplish great things in life when you have the support of others but doing these things on your own with little or no support is to be celebrated.

Maybe you don't feel that you've accomplished great things but I'm here to tell you that every day you wake up, go to work, run your business, and provide for your children, you are accomplishing something great! So again, I say to you, you are not defined by your singleness and you are not limited as a single mom. There are so many resources available to you and complete strangers who are willing to help you accomplish your goals and your dreams so keep dreaming, keep pressing forward, and keep being great!

I'm rooting for you! – Gianni

Gianni Logan is an Accounting Leader for the Louisiana division of the nation's sixth largest insurance agency, Brown & Brown Insurance.

She received an undergraduate degree in Accounting & Finance from the University of Louisiana at Lafayette and a Master of Business Administration from Texas A&M University – Commerce. Gianni's expertise in Accounting & Finance conjoined with her desire to help individuals & businesses grow led her to start her own business in December 2018.

Gianni consults with individuals and small businesses where her main objective is increasing both personal and business net income through awareness, streamlining, and reduction of expenses. She believes that individuals should adopt a business approach in their personal finances where expenses are minimized while income continually grows. Gianni also provides tax consulting to both individuals and businesses.

12

Grace for the Journey!

I grew up in a single parent home where my mother gave birth to me at the young age of eighteen. I am forever grateful for my mother and grandmother raising me and my little sister. They taught us to be independent, to work hard, get an education, love others and most importantly, to keep God first in our lives. I saw the struggles that my mother had raising my sister and I without much help from our fathers. So, as you can imagine, I was devastated when I decided to get a divorce.

The last thing that I wanted was for our children to grow up in a broken home. As a biology major, I researched the statics of children being raised in a single parent home and the odds were stacked up against us. I made the most difficult decision that I have ever made in my life when I decided to divorce my ex-husband and become a single mom. Our marriage was very toxic, and I knew that I had to get myself and our children out of that toxic environment. I made that decision prayerfully and while seeking wise counsel. During the last moments of our marriage, I didn't even recognize myself physically, emotionally, spiritually or mentally. I gained an unspeakable amount of weight. I was grieving the loss of my marriage; I was questioning God and I was severely depressed. I got married at the age of twenty-seven and I was divorced by the age of thirty-two.

At that time, my daughter was three and my son was two years old. I had no appetite and I lost over sixty pounds in only a few weeks. My heart was broken, and I was miserable. I hardly had energy to take care of myself and my children. This was a very difficult transition for my children and I. As time passed, both of my children started acting out and I gave them room to express themselves. I decided to find a therapist so they could heal properly. I found a therapist for my daughter; spoke to a few therapists and I was informed that my son was too young to benefit from therapy.

Nevertheless, if I noticed any signs of him not adjusting well as he got older, I decided I would seek out a therapist for him as well. My daughter's therapist assisted her in expressing herself through play therapy, so she could get the help that she needed, which allowed her to thrive and heal.

I too started seeing my therapist on a regular basis. My therapist helped me to understand my situation better and how to move forward. I also attended a Divorce Care class at a local church, and I made some amazing friends while taking that class. I am happy to report that my children and I are doing exceptionally well. God was with us every step of the way, even when I didn't feel like He was there or even recognized Him.

Shortly after my divorce, God instructed me to empower women, which is how MOMMY Foundation, Inc. was birthed. At MOMMY Foundation, Inc., we empower women and assist in becoming the best version of themselves. After experiencing so many recent changes, I wanted to give my children more stability, so I decided to purchase my first home. Becoming a homeowner was a major accomplishment for my children and I. They have chores and they help me with the up-keep of our home. I remind them on occasion that mommy is buying our home, but I will be leaving our home to them.

My belief in God and His promises for my life have given me the courage to make it through some very dark times in my life. When I feel discouraged, I open my Bible and I'm reminded of who he says that I am. My favorite scripture is Philippians 4:13 KJV: "I can do all things through Christ which strengthens me." So many moms ask me how I juggle it all. I've been told that "I make being a single mom look easy!" Here is a secret, God gives me strength daily to fulfill all the tasks that are on my "to-do-list." I am not perfect; I make mistakes and I can get behind on deadlines at times, but I don't make that the norm.

My children and I are on a schedule from the time we wake up till the time we go to bed; which is how I am able to stay on top of our everyday tasks such as: homework, studying, grocery shopping, self-care, family outings, spending time with friends, home, car maintenance; etc. I have a village of people who help me care for my children or give me a break when I am overwhelmed by my responsibilities.

I am forever grateful for my amazing parents, my siblings, my children's father and my genuine friends. I have gained wisdom and knowledge from attending classes, reading books to aid in my healing process and from having a relationship with God. I want to share what I have learned with others; thus, I became a life coach so that I can help others reach their goals and aid them in living their best lives.

Dear Single Mom,

Don't be too hard on yourself! Some days you will feel like you're slaying it and are on top of the world. Then there will be days you'll feel like you're the worst mom on the planet. Do yourself and your children a favor, don't beat yourself up. To your children you are the most amazing mom in the world! Take it a day at a time; even if it needs to be an hour at a time. Remember; whatever emotion that you're feeling or whatever you're facing has an expiration date.

Kinatta M. Hobbs-Vaughn graduated from Philander Smith College with a Bachelor of Biology in 2016. She is employed at Little Rock Job Corps, where she serves as the Disability/Testing Coordinator. She is the Founder and President of MOMMY Foundation, Inc.

This organization empowers mothers by offering life skills education, connecting moms to resources in their community, mentoring services and promoting self-care to ensure successful parenting. She is passionate about helping women, particularly single moms, to live their best lives.

She is the owner of *Kinatta Vaughn Transformational Life Coach Services*, where she creates her own natural skin products. She also offers Life Coach sessions and booking for motivational speaking engagements. She lives in Arkansas with her amazing daughter and son.

If you would like to connect with me, my email address is kinatta.vaughn@gmail.com and my website addresses are: https://payhip.com/KVTLCServices and https://kinatta-vaughn-transformational-life coach.ueniweb.com and you can also connect with me via Facebook at Kinatta Vaughn, or on Instagram at kinatta_tlc_bodycare.

13

Searching for Love in the Wrong Places

I used to think being a single mom was the only thing that defined my entire life, and that I could not have a future past my failures. I spent years chasing love, affection, and acceptance in many ways. I thought that I needed a man to complete my family, and this thinking got me into abusive, controlling, and manipulating situations that was not in the will of God. See, I never took the time to see what God was showing me in the mist of my mess.

In February of 2005, I found out I was going to be a mother, and in August, I gave birth to my first baby girl in Atlanta, GA. This was the scariest moment of my entire life and her father missed every moment of it. My daughter's father only saw her four times from the time she was born to the age of three, because he left us while I was pregnant. In May of 2006, I was lonely with a baby, so I met a man online who caught my eye. Soon I fell in love with him, because he shared the same name as my daughters' father and the same birthday as my daughter.

In my mind, he was "the one" and I was going to be happy. One day, I caught him in the bed with another woman and we broke it off but stayed in contact. In February 2007, I ended up pregnant again. I told him about the pregnancy, but I never told him that it was his child. I ended up giving birth in November to another baby girl and an entire year went by before I told him about her. When I did tell him about the baby, he disappeared for the next three years of her life because he was scared. When she was around four years old, he took a DNA test and it proved that he was her father. That's when he started to rebuild their relationship. The road has not been easy for all of us, but he is in her life now.

At one point in my life, I was broken and hurt by my family and looking for love a validation and I found that in my oldest daughter's father. Here I was again falling for this man but this time around, I would find so many things about him I was not ready for. Shortly after getting together, we gave birth to our son in September of 2009. I thought my life had come full circle because I had everything I always wanted. See, I was in love with this man from the age of nineteen to thirty-one years old, despite the fact he kept abandoning us. I thought he was my entire life, and he was sent to me by God but that was far from the truth.

In the years I was with him I had been treated as if I was replaceable, talked down to, and disrespected in so many ways. All this while also being told I was special to him and he loved me, and I was his "Queen." I remember working doubles at work for weeks on end while his parents raised our kids. There were times where I was begging him to watch our kids while I worked and paying him $100 to do it. Things like this and worst happened for years with this man.

Women he was sleeping with meeting my children while we were together, picking me up late from work, telling me to "play my part" and not complain. There were so many toxic signs of mental and verbal abuse for years with this man and I ignored them because my children having their dad in their lives was more important to me. In May of 2016, this man left me and my children again for another woman and her family. That was the year I was done, and I left Atlanta and moved home to Philadelphia. I was blessed with an apartment and began to rebuild my life, but I was still looking for love.

I met a man, and I spent months getting to know him and spending time with him and his daughters. For four months, I spent time with him on a strictly platonic level until one day I made the mistake of taking it to another level and ended up pregnant. From the day I told him about my pregnancy, he revealed himself and I was told I was nothing but trash, and my daughter would never have a father no matter how hard I tried. On April 30, 2018, my daughter was born, and that moment change my life for the best. I realized that I spent years looking for love in all the wrong places and that God had so much in store for my life. That year, I realized I did not need a man in my life to find purpose in who I was.

So, in August, I started school with four children and not a clue about my next move and in December of 2020

I finished, because I trusted God and believed in myself. Men counted me out, family counted me out and even some friends counted me out, BUT GOD!!! I have achieved more in those two years than I have achieved in my entire life looking for a man to complete me.

Dear Single Mom,

Do not look for validation in places that will have you questioning who or whose you are. For me, I trust on Proverbs 3:5-6 that says, "Trust in the Lord with all your heart and lean not on your own understanding, in all thy ways acknowledge him, and he shall direct your path."

When each of these men and family failed or turned their backs, God has always been in my corner. Each time I relied on my faith in God, doors opened, and my family has always been taken care of.

Che'ne' Robinson is a Graduate of Harrisburg Area Community College with her degree in Early Childhood Education and an inspiring spiritual life coach. This Philadelphia native started Light of Minds Early Learning Academy in September 2017 after realizing she wanted to make a difference in her community.

This mom has been a single mom for fifteen years after being connected to many people who have told her what she could not do. She has overcome homelessness, emotional and mental abuse, and raising her four children with little to no help. Ms. Robinson is an inspiration to many women and children whom she is in direct contact with, and she enjoys changing lives for the better. You can follow her on IG: @Chene_Robinson Or Facebook at: Chene Robinson

14

Don't Lose You

Life does not stop after you have children. It took me a while to finally wrap my head around that concept. Actually, it took the help of my ex mother-in-law to help realize that my kids, her grandchildren, did not need me twenty-four hours a day. That it was okay for me to have a life outside of them.

When I divorced my kids' father, I felt like they were all I had in this world. My entire world revolved around my two kids. If it did not involve those two, nothing else really mattered to me. My focus was making sure I was doing everything in my power to be the best mom I could be. Everything was about them no matter what. It was getting to the point where I would always get that "inner guilt" if I ever considered doing something for myself. I felt like a selfish mother at times. It was pretty bad.

I could be in the store ready to buy a few things for myself and then I would end up putting it back because in my mind, I had kids to take care of and I really didn't need that new shirt or pair of pants. I would rarely go out. All I would do was be home with my kids. In the process of doing that, I lost myself or maybe I never knew myself to begin with. People can be a distraction. What I mean by that is, sometimes you are so wrapped up in other individuals that you do not have to deal with your own personal issues.

God knows I love my kids dearly, but I was beginning to think, *"Is this all I'm going to do with myself? Raise kids?"* Then, every so often, my kids' grandmother's words would always come back to me. "Your kids don't need you twenty-four hours a day." She has always been a big supporter of me even after me and her son divorced. She always encouraged me to have a life of my own. Slowly, I began to do things on my own. Just enjoying myself.

You must learn to do things outside of your kids. If you do not, once those kids are grown and gone, you will not know what to do with yourself. I have seen it one too many times where a parent, mostly single mothers, has invested all their years to raising their children and now that those kids are grown, they have a hard time letting go. Those type of relationships can go left real quick because some mothers, not all, have this idea that their kids owe them something or they find themselves always in the midst of their kids' lives, not allowing them to just be free. I believe a lot of that stems from us mothers not having anything for ourselves in the process of raising them. That type of relationship can be toxic. If I am honest with myself, I could see myself behaving that way had I not started doing things for me and me only.

A few months back, me and my daughter were sitting around talking about my future in the military. I was telling her that I am close to the point in which I can retire, and I was considering doing it. She looked at me and said, "Why?" She was like, "You said you always wanted to retire as a Senior Master Sergeant, and I think you should go for it." She meant "Chief," but I knew what she meant. Her response surprised me because I thought my kids would be happier if I were able to be at home with them more. Her comments only revealed to me that your kids want you to achieve your goals just as much as you want them to achieve theirs. Your children will not hate you for wanting to do things outside of them. Often times, they will be your biggest supporters.

Dear Single Mom,

Being a single parent does not mean putting your life on hold to raise your kids. All your kids really want from you is for you to love them, cherish them, and to be there for them when they need. None of those things require you to put the things you want to achieve in life on hold.

You are a beautiful powerful woman whom God has placed purpose on the inside of you to bring forth. God didn't just put you on this earth just to raise children. You being a mother is only part of God's plan for you. Do not allow your current situation to keep you sitting on the gifts/purpose that God has given you. Be blessed and stay the course that is mapped out for you.

Angela R. Sharp was born and raised in Little Rock, AR. Shortly after graduating Sylvan Hills High School, she joined the United States Air Force. She is divorcee with two kids, Ardrianna and James.

She also has a stepson, Steven Jr. Angela is also a graduate of Ashford University. She published her first novel, *Why Didn't You Love Me* in the fall of 2019. Her second novel, *Consequences* was released in the summer of 2020. Her desire is to inspire people to always strive to be the best person that God created them to be. Angela resides in New Mexico where she remains on active duty with the Air Force.

15

"It's All for a Purpose!"

Now the cute part is over! The baby shower, the baby bump pictures and my mama at my side getting everything I needed to feel "comfortable." I have this beautiful baby that I'm finally able to meet and kiss and love on. Let's get real, I'm feeling alone. Now what? It's just me and the baby. I wish I would've known that God equipped me already and God never makes mistakes. See, I was pregnant by twenty-three thinking I made it! I made it past my friends, and I beat statistics. I'm good!

But, I really didn't know what I was doing. All my friends were on baby number two and they had life down packed with the first kid. So, there I was in a one-bedroom apartment with my child's father. I was trying to play this role of a mother from what I saw my mother do and what I saw on television. I didn't know three years later I'd be alone in a relationship taking care of everything like a man should.

So I left, mentally. Although I was still there physically, I had made up in my head that this relationship will not change. I stood on my two feet and went to work. I was broken into pieces due to being verbally abused. By January 1, 2018, I made the decision to be happy no matter what. I isolated myself and did the work. I discovered my self-worth, I got baptized and went through the healing process. I started to serve in church and made like-minded friends. I enrolled my daughter to get a Christian education that grew her relationship with God.

I begin to see a change in her behavior and her as a child, in general. Things seem so good for a while until the end of 2019. We finally moved from my mom's home into a house of our own and I landed a good job. Then, all of a sudden, it seemed as if all hell broke loose. By the end of the month of August 2019 I was let go from my job and was stuck with all kind of bills. I was still trying to maintain our home and keep things intact. My daughter was not able to continue attending her Christian school and was forced to go to public school where she experienced bullying.

Everything was spiraling out of control! I was over everything at this point. After another setback, I ran for the hills, literally! I needed a fresh start, badly. I thought about the plan I wanted since a young adult and before my child. A plan to reside somewhere in Georgia at some point in life. One day on my way home, after being terminated from another job, I had a long walk. While walking, I made the decision to get us out of Texas, by any means.

After some planning, I decided to start fresh. I was leaving our present life behind. I took clothes as well as small, sentimental things and we left for the hills. Pre-pandemic, I was on the way to Georgia with no job, no place to call my own but with faith the size of a mustard seed. My friend from Texas allowed me one month to get a job and a place to live. So, here I was, from a three-bedroom home to a friend's floor with my eight-year-old.

The pandemic made it hard to find work. By the time the thirty days was up, we transitioned to an extended stay hotel. I still had faith through it all but was still thinking, "I am crazy!" I made a hard decision to let my daughter go back to Texas for the summer. I had to roll my sleeves up and get my hands dirty to do whatever it took to provide a living for us in Georgia. The day we left for Texas, I got a call from a job to do a phone interview to work from home. I was hired that day and started working within days; three days! Just like that, things were turning around.

On my way back to Georgia, I was still homeless, by this time, everyone I knew had their stimulus check but me. I woke up to an email with a notification that my stimulus check was in my post office box waiting on me. Within seven days, I had a townhouse apartment and a job. In 90 days, I was working and living in Georgia and all felt well. The peace I have now is like no other. My peace is from God and not of this world.

I wanted to come to Georgia because I knew God would get the glory from it all. I was tired of being in this victimized situation and not being able to provide fully for my daughter. I knew coming to Georgia would force me to lean on God for everything and strip me of all distractions. He continues to provide and show his faithfulness.

Dear Single Mom,

I want to tell you the only way to wholeness is God. I was taught about God but not how to have a relationship with Him. When I experienced a real encounter with God, my daughter was six years old. That's when I realized that all of what I went and was going through was for a reason. My endless nights of no sleep, many nights of crying and nights I couldn't see her because I was working late. Let's be honest, the nights I was out late just trying to find out who I was as a woman. Those moments gave me healing! Once you find your worth and identity in Christ, you'll see it was all a part of His plan for your good and His glory.

Jeretta Emanuel was born and raised on the southside of Houston, TX and now resides in Marietta, GA with her eight-year-old daughter.

By day, she's an Administrative Assistant, and by night, she's the owner of *Purpose Chasin*, a Christian apparel company that focuses on chasing after the purpose God gave us. As a woman of God who loves to laugh and make others laugh, Jeretta's clothing reflects the same spirit by displaying vibrant, positive faith-based messages. In her spare time, she loves to play in makeup, watch YouTube tutorials, listen to music, read and spend time with family and friends.

16

Dear Single Mom

Before becoming a single mother, I was in an abusive marriage for five years. I met my ex-husband at a church I attended for over a year. He loved to worship God just like I do, and he was kind and gentle. I assumed he was perfect for me; heck, he was "Brother Tony." Shortly after we got married, the verbal abuse began and intensified through the years of our marriage. In year four, I began to have dreams of him stabbing me to death; I had that dream four different times. I finally cried out to God and said, "I thought you loved me. I have already been through so much. Why would you let me marry him? I asked you if he was my husband."

God immediately dropped His answer into my spirit saying, "Yes, you did ask me if he was your husband, but you did not wait for my answer." God's response to me was sobering because he was right. I did not wait on his answer. I immediately repented and my follow up question to Him was, "Ok, so what now Lord?" Over the next several weeks, God revealed to me that if I did not leave that marriage that man was going to kill me. That was enough for me. I knew that I had God's approval to remove myself from that marriage. So, I took a blank large canvas, some stencils and paint and put DELIVER US on the canvas. I then hung the painting on the wall in our living room. That was my declaration to God. That painting was a symbol of my trust in God and readiness to move forward.

Now, at this time, we had three small children. They were three, two and one. I had no money in savings, no family or friends to turn to and absolutely no idea how I was going to provide for three children on my own. But I made a decision to trust God. About a week after hanging that painting, my ex-husband began to have intense tooth pains. He was in such pain he was bed ridden. Within this same time, God dropped into my spirit to call my local domestic violence shelter. I did as instructed, I called the hotline, informed them of what was going on and how many children I had.

I was informed that they had room for me and my children. They directed me to collect all our important paperwork if I was able and to report to the nearest police department to be escorted to the facility. At this domestic violence shelter and many of them throughout the country, they require a police escort to the facility because the safe havens are in non-disclosed locations for the safety of all women and children that reside there.

Within twenty-four hours, I was able to gather all the essentials we needed i.e., clothes, shoes, birth certificates, social security cards and so forth. Because my ex was so preoccupied by his pain, my children and I were able to make it out undetected. We stayed at the shelter for three months. On the third month, the shelter helped move me and my children into a nice place of our own and paid our rent for three months. I did not have a job when we first moved into our place.

I can recall spending many nights crying out to God asking Him how I was going to be able to maintain our new place and provide for my children. Putting my children in daycare and working a nine-to-five was not a viable option for me. My babies had already been through so much with moving away from their dad, going into a shelter and moving into a new place. I did not feel it wise to have them away from me all day.

In this dilemma, I decided to start a business that I could run from home while home schooling my little ones. My expertise is sales, so I started a company as a sales consultant. I remember many nights sitting at my laptop fleshing the company out and crying as I boldly set out to become a successful entrepreneur. Each night and day I would ask wisdom to provide to me the strategy I needed to bring in right clients for my business.

Within a couple weeks of doing this, I woke up one morning with an entire strategy laying on top of me... that's what it felt like anyways. After getting my children situated, I got right to work on the strategy. Less than a month later, I was able to bring in two clients that, combined, paid me the same amount I made in my highest paying executive sales position in Corporate America. Within a six-month period, I brought in $40,000 and I was absolutely astonished by how well God had provided for my family and me. This success led me on a path that never ever returned me to be employed by anyone. I have

been adjusting, grinding, failing and succeeding as a businesswoman ever since.

Dear Single Mom,

No matter what you are facing right now, you do not need to have all the answers. You simply need to inquire of and trust in the one who does--God. If you are in an abusive relationship, even if it is your marriage, God desires so much more for you. Victory is your portion. When you allow yourself to trust God and step out in faith, you will embark on a journey that will be satisfying to your soul and to your pocketbook. God will provide.

Shakena Renee Luster is a seer, inspirational speaker, author, screenwriter, and reality television show creator. She recently released her debut novel, "The Prophet" and then went on to turn that novel into a screenplay. She is currently pitching her new TV show concept to production companies. This charismatic, fiery, sweetheart was born in Cleveland, OH and raised in Colorado Springs, CO. She has a passion for speaking into the broken places of women. Everything she creates is anchored in deliverance and inspiration for those who need to be set free.

17

Child of Mine

I loved you unconditionally as anyone could see!!!

Loving you too much only hurts me!!!

I have been there for you through it all.

At times, it seems my best is not good enough, for you at all.

I gave to you when no one else would!

I've prayed for you when no one else could!

I've stood for you when no one else cared.

Child of mine your mother will all always be there!

I've made decisions that I thought were the best for you!!! To protect and guide you to make a better future for you. Never in a million years would I ever harm you. Child of mine, for your mother will always be there by your side. I tried to show you how to love the ones who loved you unconditionally. To give back love in return I'm not talking to all three. But I raised you all the right way and someday you'll see, it was the best way for you to reach your destiny. For child of mine, your mother will always be by your side.

1996- There were some people who wanted my parents to put me out because I was pregnant, but I had some awesome parents who supported my son and I every step of the way. I was only nineteen years old and was scared because this little person was depending on me to take care of him. People talked about me especially the church folk. My family was there to help and without them I don't know how we would have made it.

I worked for a little while but the money I made around here was pennies to me. I needed more, so I enlisted into the US Army to provide a better life for my son and I. I was enlisted for three and a half years, with plans on bringing my son with me, not knowing that I had to be married or have some type of living arrangement for him to be able to live with me. So on the first and the fifteenth, I was sending money home to take care of business. A few years passed and I met my first husband. We got married and we brought my son to Texas.

2000- After the birth of my second son, I decided I didn't want to raise my children as "Army Brats." I "ETS" (expiration-term of service) out of the military and moved back home. We moved in with my parents for a couple of months, but I was grown and needed my own space. Sometimes men don't understand that when your grown you need your space and can't live with your parents!!!! By this time my marriage was in shambles, so we separated. I found a little apartment for the children and I. I enrolled in a medical college to become a medical assistant so I could get a better paying job.

In 2002, I became pregnant with my daughter. I was in my mid-twenties and by this time I was in a very dark place in my life, but it didn't stop me from taking care of my children. I was on government assistance: housing, daycare, and food stamps my children. I had multiple jobs, I worked at Wal- Mart on the night shift for about two months before I quit. I worked at a daycare, a doctor's office, and I sat with the mentally challenged.

For a while, I worked two jobs and sometimes three to keep the bills paid. It's truly a gift and a blessing from God to be a mother. It is also a blessing to have such wonderful children. At times, I really wanted to give up and throw in the towel when things got rough, but I knew I couldn't because there were three little people depending on me to survive. I thank God for giving me my children when He gave them to me. They helped pull me out of some dark places in my life. They gave me a reason to smile when I didn't feel like smiling and a reason to push when I didn't feel like pushing.

I had to sacrifice for my children which wasn't a problem. The only thing that got under my skin was being called a "gold-digging baby mama" for making their fathers do their part after I'd given them chances to take care of their children before putting them on child support. I tried to work with them and help them out, but it didn't work!! God bless them anyway!!! I thank God for wisdom knowledge and understanding to you that these men don't know any better and they need help!!!

Dear Single Mom,

Please keep your head up and know that the sacrifices you are making for your children aren't in vain.

Karen Dunomes is a single parent of three children, Tiyler Charleston, Lance Todd, Jr., and Samoria Rayven. She attended Hammond High which she graduated from in 1995. After graduation she attended Southeastern. In 1996-2001 she joined the US Army.

After ETS out of the Military, she attended Medical College in Baton Rouge and she was certified as a Phlebotomist. After attending Medical College, she attended Compass Career College for medical assistant. She worked at Options for about two years as a caretaker. After that She worked at the Blood Center for eight years as a supervisor. Currently, she works at XPO logistics. She is a member of New Creation OMC of Hammond, LA.

You can follow her @ Karen Dunomes

Kae2sam- Instagram

18

Unbalanced Scales

Here is a story about a mother who thought dedicating her entire existence to raising her child, found the error in that way of thinking and how it put her in a position of almost emotional destruction. I made a wrong turn, assuming that if I avoided what hurt me that would help my child. It took a decade before I learned that healing my trauma was the first step in giving my child a chance at combating the same predispositions.

I desired more for her. I did not want her to feel the level of pain I did, so I worked myself into an emotional oblivion trying to protect her. That mindset, "I want more for my child than I had," can be damaging if everything we do for them is from a fragmented mental space. Of course, we want more, but failing to heal what brought you to that frame of mind will only give them more of the very things we fail to heal within ourselves.

At conception, you have all of your egg cells, so your mother's trauma passed to you and your seed. Let's not forget the fact that the father's trauma is passed to the child as well, through the memory carried in his semen. Quadruple whammy! I had a front-row seat watching this play out between my daughter and me, so I beseech you to heal and live.

All of my adult life, I have been a mother. Before my twenty-first birthday, I had a beautiful baby girl named Cayla. My daughter was fourteen years old before I started to live and discover who I am. Before that, I devoted myself to her because I grew up feeling like my parents chose their intimate partners over me. This devotion was to avoid running the risk of doing the same thing my parents did.

After spending most of my daughter's life single, I started dating only to hear her say those dreadful words: "She chose him over me." I thought that if I put myself on the back burner to make sure my child was exemplary in every area, I was doing the right thing as a parent. I did not want to be one of those parents who expected others to raise my child while I found myself or "ran the streets." Despite how much we want to do things differently, without healing, subconsciously, we play out the same life.

I chose to become invisible; I decided to snuff out my passion, I decided to bottle the essence of my being and bury it in a time capsule because I thought that anything else would label me a bad mother. I gave everything, every part of me, until I had no more. I died so she could live. What I was doing was not healthy for either of us; the scales were unbalanced. Our upbringings were on different ends of the spectrum, but each end was laced with traumas that ultimately met in the middle.

In a state of brokenness, I would attack first and talk later when it came to my child. I knew the pain of being bullied by adults, so I didn't play when it came to her. However, that caused my child to withhold information from me. A teacher retaliated because of my rebuttal to her disrespect, so my child feared telling me when she was emotionally traumatized by adults.

Upon finding out, I felt like a failure—the way I responded in her defense was because the little girl in me did not have it when a teacher lined up an entire class to sniff me as I laid my head on the desk wanting to die. The teacher was convinced I smelled, and everyone needed to smell what she smelled. That traumatized little girl rose to defend Cayla—the little girl who had no one to stand up for her. I tried my best to be this perfect mother. My child never lacked anything, she had me and everything she desired. Her godmother would tell me all the time to stop overcompensating but I did not fully understand at the time what she was saying.

At a young age, I saw a gift in her and began to cultivate it in any way possible. I was the happiest mother ever to start a business for my daughter and put her in various programs to develop her gift. I was no baker, but she baked with excellence. She ran her company for a few years before she closed it, citing I was why the desire faded and that she never really wanted any of it.

During this time, I was in therapy, soul detoxing, attending coaching sessions, building a brand, authoring a book, I was finally living, but to my daughter, my entire existence was a problem. That pain I cannot put into words. When choosing me, I became the villain, and the very ones who awaited my demise were glad about it. I hardly received help raising my child, but since I was the mutual enemy, the support on her behalf manifested quickly. I was in yet another battle because despite how things were going, I had to save my child from the mind-sets that nearly destroyed me.

Although I was healing, the generational trauma came to collect. Eventually, my daughter and I got to a point where we could hear one another. Initially, she refused to counsel because a family member advised her against it; but she understood the necessity. Both of us were healing so that we can rebuild. That experience had to happen for the reconstruction to be on a better foundation. We had to experience the demolition before the remodel. There was a lot we both needed to learn and areas we both had to grow in. Healing is continual, but we both have committed to bonding from a whole place rather than a fragmented one.

Dear Single Mom,

Heal thyself, heal your family, and balance those scales.

LaToya Nicole is a best-selling author, life coach, personal development counselor, organizer, and owner of S.O.L.O. Coaching & Consulting LLC in Baton Rouge, LA.

She is a passionate coach and consultant with a zest for success and living life by design. She helps individuals who are stagnant, process setbacks in a healthy way in order to move forward in purpose. As a success enthusiast, she prides herself on maintaining mental health and emotional intelligence.

She is aligned continuously to her vision, and healing organizationally. In the future, she plans to author more books, start a nonprofit assisting youth in processing pain through the arts, host retreats and develop wellness communities.

For more information, visit her website www.solocoaching.net

To connect with her, send an email to latoyanicole@solocoaching.net

Say Hello On:

Twitter: @sheislatoya

Instagram: @iamlatoyanicole_ and @goingsolo_llc

Facebook: LaToya Nicole

19

"Don't Stop!"

Thursday, August 22, 2013 is the day that changed my life. I became a mother to a beautiful, healthy baby girl. This should have been an exciting time for me. But back then, at the age of twenty-eight, a full-grown woman, whose father was a Baptist preacher, I was scared! I had my entire life planned out. I had plans to graduate from Southeastern Louisiana University with my Bachelor of Early Childhood Education, complete Grad School before the age of thirty, get married and receive my Ph.D. in Curriculum and Instruction by thirty-five.

I had it all figured out…not! I never dreamed that I would become a single mom. I was so ashamed because I felt that I let my family down. I wanted to be the first girl to graduate college and to make my parents proud. But instead, I became the girl who had premarital sex with a married man and have just given birth to his child. I knew my life was over; that the chances of being successful at anything, was slim to none.

For the first few months after having my daughter, I was an emotional wreck. I was fighting so many battles at once. I was stressed out having to provide for my child alone, the feeling of guilt and shame, my daughter's father not being accepting of her, on top of hormones being out of whack! I would binge eat and cry all the time. I remember one day going into the kitchen while my mother was cooking, and with tears in my eyes I said, "I think I may have post-partum depression."

My mother stopped what she was doing and began praying for me. She rebuked the enemy and began declaring life over me; that I will be successful, I am a great mother, I am strong, and that my life belongs to the almighty God. I immediately felt the weight of stress being lifted. That day, she gave the devil a good "Deebo beatdown" and took his gold chain!

Now, I would love to say after that day things got better… It didn't. For the next two years, I found myself in a power struggle because I still wasn't at the place where I thought I should be. I was a preschool teacher at an Early Learning Center, and I desired to finished school, but God had other plans. I found myself failing course after course which made me become discouraged. God was trying to get my attention, but I didn't want to see it!

Then the unthinkable happened. In November 2016, my mother was diagnosed with Stage II Bladder Cancer. Five months later, on April 10, 2017, she lost her battle. This was the darkest time of my life because not only did I lose my mother, my best friend… I lost my foundation. It was like someone pulled the rug from under me! I was lost. I thought I wasn't good enough to take care of my daughter alone. At times I became overwhelmed with the responsibilities of being a mom and wanted to give up.

Not having enough money to make ends meet, trying to finish school, and needing God to do a miracle in my life had become a heavy weight. I often asked God the question, when will I have my "parting the Red Sea" moment and walk across on dry ground? What I was seeing wasn't where I thought I should be! But God reminded me of one of my favorite scriptures, Jeremiah 29:11 (MSG) that says, "I know what I am doing. I have it all planned out—plans to take care of you, not abandon you, plans to give you the future you hope for."

This scripture kept me from giving up when I was battling with depression and thoughts of suicide. It encouraged me to keep pushing to be the best I can be, that God knows what he's doing, he cares about me to make sure that everything will work for my good, and that regardless of what it looks like, my future is brighter because he has given me an expected end!

In 2018, God began dealing with me about entrepreneurship and multiple streams of income. This became my new dream! I began praying and believing in the promises of God. He began giving me visions of who I will become and dared me to declare and believe that He will do it. He led me to the scripture, Mark 11:23-24 – "I shall have whatever I say if I pray and believe that I will receive them!" At that moment, I realized, "Wow, God! That's a promise!"

So, I began to dream big! Within two years, I am beginning to see the vision being manifested. I am so glad that I didn't give up. I can proudly say that I am a nationally Certified Childcare Director, recently state Certified Child Care Health Consultant, and owner of Monarch Beauty Supply which all will bring in multiple streams of income. I am so grateful that God has given me the strength and grace to endure the challenges, to pursue my dreams, and to defy the odds.

Dear Single Mom,

Don't beat yourself up because where you are, isn't where you think you should be. You are where God wants you to be. Don't allow yourself to be discouraged by how far you must go but look in the rearview mirror of your life and see how far you have come. I implore you, don't stop when you begin to feel frustrated.

Don't stop when things get hard and you can't see how it's going to work out. Don't stop when the resources are not there. Don't stop when no one is supporting you. Don't stop when people question the vision God has given you. Don't stop because the vision has not manifested. Don't stop but keep pressing towards the mark. The finish line is just ahead!

Pamela Williams is a native of Bogalusa, Louisiana, and a single mother of one. She actively serves as Secretary at The Kingdom of God Church.

Pamela is also a preschool teacher at AppleTREE Academy where she has taught for seven years. An advocate for children, Pamela supports early learning centers and head start programs who effectively build learning foundations for young children. With 14 years of teaching experience, Pamela holds a CDA (Child Development Associate) Credential, Ancillary Certification, National Administration Credential through NECPA (National Early Childhood Program Accreditation), is state certified as a CCHC (Child Care Health Consultant) by the Louisiana Department of Health, and has recently became owner of Monarch Beauty Supply, LLC.

You can visit www.monarchbeautysupply.com,
follow on Facebook @MonarchBeautySupply
or email monarchbeautysupply@zohomail.com.

20

When Tragedy Strikes

Being a single mother is tough. I'm sure you know that, right? Of course, you do. But even in its toughness, it has its rewards. There is no better feeling in this whole wide world than watching and witnessing a milestone or celebrating an accomplishment or achievement with your children. It makes you forget about all the hardships you endured to get to that moment. It makes you realize that the struggle was worth it and that you can do ANYTHING you put your mind to. Sometimes, it takes a tragedy to hit us before realizing that we are a lot stronger than we think. Here's what I mean.

Anyone who knows me knows that my mom was my everything. We didn't have the best relationship, but she was my world. We disagreed on many things, but I NEVER let it get in the way of my love for her. She was always right, no matter what. That's just the way she was. My mom suffered from hypertension, diabetes, and heart disease brought on by excessive years of smoking. She battled with quitting for a while, but she finally stopped when her health issues became more frequent. I cared for her when her problems started to get a little worse. I became a full-time mother and caregiver. I made sure she went to all of her appointments, scheduled the appointments, handled all of her affairs, all while being a full-time single mom. I held it all together, even as her health started to decline.

My mother developed a sore under the toe of her right foot. By her being a diabetic, she never knew that it was there until it started to bother her. She asked my oldest daughter to look at it for her, and once my daughter saw the severity of it, she immediately called me. I was in Las Vegas, attending a business seminar for a network marketing company that I was working for at the time. She told me that I needed to take my mom to the doctor when I returned because it looked really bad. I asked her to FaceTime me to see what I would be dealing with when I returned home.

When she did, I, too, recognized the severity of it. It looked as if my mom had stepped on something, and it had broken the skin. The skin was white and torn from her foot. I knew that I would have to do a lot of convincing to get her to let me take her to the doctor when I got home. I knew that she would not go quietly into the night and would put up a fight. What I didn't realize is that this would be the beginning of the end. If I had known, I would've done things differently.

When I returned home from my trip, I scheduled a doctor's appointment for my mom to see the doctor and figure out what needed to be done to heal her foot. She didn't go. I scheduled several more appointments, all of which she missed. It was very frustrating, and her foot was getting worse. So was her health, but I never noticed because I was more concerned about getting her foot healed. When she got to the point where she could barely put weight on the foot and was hurting badly to the point that she could barely walk, she finally went to the doctor. I was excited because I thought that she would begin a journey of healing, and we could move on to something else. How wrong I was.

When we made it to the hospital, we learned that her toe was infected, and the infection began to spread. The doctor said that her toes had to be amputated. Simple right? Wrong! A few days before the scheduled amputation, she developed a blood clot in her hips. They had to go in and take care of that before they amputated the toes. The procedure was done a week later, and that's when her health slowly started to decline. She developed an infection in her lungs, and they became inflamed. Her oxygen levels began to drop, and there were days where she couldn't hold her own oxygen without the help of a mini bi-pap machine. She started eating less and less and wasn't putting out any feces or urine. She became tired and weak, and all she wanted to do was sleep. She begged for water, but we couldn't give her any because she couldn't swallow anymore without choking, and it made her oxygen levels drop dramatically. She was suffering, and I could see it. I hated every moment of it.

On May 22, 2019, my mom gained her wings. She passed the day after my second daughter's fourteenth birthday. It was the worst day of our lives. My children were close to my mom, so it hit them extra hard. She helped me raise them. We never thought she would leave us, not at the tender age of sixty-eight. She still had her whole life ahead of her. She was my rock, my best friend. And now, she was gone.

I wrote her obituary while helping my girls stay focused in school. I wanted to quit everything. My job, the beginning of my writing career, EVERYTHING. After we buried her, she came and let me know that she was okay and was in a better place. She told me that she would always be with us and that she loved me and was very proud of me. I felt better after that visit from her. She let me know that she was at peace, and that gave me a sense of peace.

It has been almost two years since her passing. I have days where I don't want to be bothered, I get depressed and cry all day, but I still do what I need to do to make sure my daughters are healthy and happy. I adjust my crown and keep it moving, just as you should. Everything is going to be okay. Believe that.

Dear Single Mom,

You are strong, beautiful, and powerful. You can do

whatever you want in this life. No matter what loss you are experiencing or have experienced in the past, use it as a stepping-stone to get where you want to be. You can do it. I am rooting for you.

Diane Parker is the mother of three beautiful daughters. They reside in Hammond, Louisiana. She works as a Certified Nursing Assistant and has been doing so for thirteen years. She attends Delgado Community College, where she is obtaining her associate's degree in Registered Nursing. She plans on attending Southern University to earn her bachelor's degree in Nursing as well.

She is the owner-operator of AKC Accommodations, where she provides her consumers with incredible savings on their travel needs, such as hotel rooms, rental cars, and cruises. Her goals are to mentor and teach women world-wide how to become successful entrepreneurs and how to build successful businesses. She also wants to become a life coach. She plans to write more books to boost her writing career.

Email: dmparker81@gmail.com
Facebook: www.facebook.com/diane.parker3
Business Site: home.ibuumerang.com

21 Untapped Strength

When I was a little girl, I thought I would grow up, get married, and have five children. At the time it seemed like a pretty logical number. My mother had five children, so I thought I would have five children. I would have a big house, my husband would be the most amazing man ever, and my kids would be perfect! I had it all planned out. Man was I surprised!

Becoming pregnant at twenty-one and pregnant at thirty out of wedlock, was not the plan. Chile, having two different baby daddies, most definitely wasn't the plan! When I became a mother, my life began to shift. I was now responsible for two human beings. I couldn't just think about myself anymore. So here I am at the tender age of forty-two, still not married and with no big house. Plenty of nights I thought to myself, "MY GOD where did I go wrong?" I mean I can't say that my life is bad, but it sure isn't the way I imagined it would be.

I am thankful to have grown and gone through life with my two favorite people. My daughter Destini who is twenty and my son Braylen who is twelve. Having two kids with such a big age gap can be difficult at times. I've had to come to grips with the fact that Destini is an adult, who wants to do adult things. On the other hand, Braylen will soon be a teenager, discovering who he will become. I am constantly trying to make sure they are both happy. I always try to make sure I give them equal time.

I have been on this single motherhood journey for the last twenty years. It has not been easy, but it has been very rewarding. There are days when I am tired, frustrated, stressed, and overwhelmed because I feel like I am all alone. There are days when it becomes so overwhelming that I want to quit, but I have to keep pushing because I have two people depending on me.

When my oldest was conceived, I can say I was not in a bad place, but I wasn't in a good place either. I was young and I wasn't making a lot of money. Her father and I weren't in a good space. While I was pregnant with my daughter, there was another female pregnant at the same time. She gave birth to her daughter, three months before I gave birth to mine. I experienced all types of emotions. I was excited because she was my first child and a girl at that.

I was nervous, and fearful about being a single mother, but nevertheless, it was too late to turn back. I would love her and nurture her the best that I could. We would grow and learn together for the next eight years until my son was born. My son's father and I were together at the time. It made things a little easier, but not that much easier.

Parenting is not an easy job, especially when you are doing it alone. Needless to say, it has been a journey for me and my children. Some days are easier than others. I haven't always made the best decisions. I haven't always operated to my fullest capacity. I haven't always been financially stable. I haven't always felt like dragging myself out of bed and parenting. And I haven't always considered myself a great mom. I get tired, angry, frustrated, and stressed out. But at the end of the day, I strive to make myself a better person for them and me.

I think of all those times when I felt like I was truly struggling to be a good mom. I had so much chaos in my heart back then and honestly, I am still challenged by those thoughts today. The difference today is I know they are just thoughts, and I see them differently.

I never gave up, I never gave in. I chose to keep at it. I made a lot of mistakes, but I never let those mistakes define my future. I knew when I decided to be a mother at twenty-one, I was going to do everything I could to make them happy. That meant finding out who I was and showing up for them no matter what, even when I did not feel up to it.

As I look back over my life, there have been many failed attempts. I tried to succeed in obtaining my college degree many times. I've tried to be a business owner for the last decade. There were things I didn't know then that I know now. There's a time for everything, but some things can't be rushed. I overcame some major struggles. Struggles that no one knew except my children and me.

Through it all, they've been my biggest supporters. I will do anything within my power to make sure they have the life they so richly deserve.

Dear Single Mom:

Are you out there feeling like you're not a good parent? Take a moment, step back, and look how far you've come. In spite of the obstacles you've faced, you have survived! You never gave up. You kept pushing. If no one else is proud of you, your children are, and I am too. Keep growing and thriving. You're doing an amazing job.

Sabrina Willis "Motivating Women to Slay with Confidence" is the creator of She Can Network, a platform used to help women regain their self-confidence after going through past traumatic experiences.

Sabrina was born in Youngstown, Ohio, but she was raised in St. Augustine, Florida. To appreciate the She Can Network, you must understand the woman behind it, and everything that she has gone through. During the time of her darkest season, Sabrina did not always have the type of support that she long for, which is why she now values community and intimate relationships. Sabrina struggled with low confidence and low self-esteem issues, which was the root cause of her ending up in toxic relationships.

Sabrina continues her journey with many followers, providing a clear and practical blueprint for personal success, drawn directly from life experiences, such as feeling stuck in life and having no idea how to move forward.

Her transparency helps so many women to see that she's been there and done that!

Her Network is a community that helps you understand that no matter what you are going through you are NEVER alone, and her goal in life is to help women become the woman, who says SHE CAN!

Connect Socially:
Follow her on Facebook@ Sabrina Willis
Follow her on Instagram@ Sabrina Willis_
Join her Network
@https://www.facebook.com/groups/SheCanNetwork/
Visit her @ SabrinaInspires.com
Email her @ SabrinaWillisllc.com

22

Curse Breaker

On my eighteenth birthday, I found out that I was pregnant for the third time. I was both excited and terrified at the news. I was excited because I had the opportunity to have the baby I always dreamt about. However, I was extremely terrified because I had been pregnant twice before and experienced child loss with both babies.

I lost my first daughter due to organ failure. She was born three months too soon and lived only fifteen days. One year later, I became pregnant again, but went into labor at twenty weeks. I found out that I suffered from a rare condition called placenta abruption. The condition causes the placenta to detach from the uterus which causes the baby to be deprived of oxygen. When I gave birth to her, she was stillborn.

The task of burying two children within twelve months took an extreme toll on my mental and emotional health. So when I found out that I was pregnant again, my anxiety went through the roof!

Fear flooded the confines of my mind!

I was nervous about telling my parents, who were for sure over it by this time.

I was afraid for my mental health, because I couldn't endure another loss.

I was terrified for the wellbeing of my unborn baby.

It was all too much!!! After losing my children, thankfully, I found God and learned how to seek Him and pray for myself. I knew I'd need to lean on Him for strength to face the uncertainty ahead. I also knew that stress could cause preterm labor, so I was intentional about removing anything and anyone who threatened my peace.

The first person to go was my baby's father. He proved early on that he wasn't going to be consistent, so I did us both a favor, and kept my distance. I quickly adjusted to doing things on my own. Due to a history of preterm labor, I was under strict doctor's orders. I had two doctors, an OBGYN and a specialist. I would visit both every other week for ultrasounds and check-ups.

At sixteen weeks, the doctor suggested that I have a procedure which involved stitching the cervix in attempts to prevent early labor. The procedure was painless, and I was hopeful that my baby would have a better chance as a result of it. Things were going well with the pregnancy then my worst nightmare came true. I went into preterm labor again!!! This time, I was thirty-two weeks, so I knew that my son had a greater chance of survival as he was more developed than the other babies. Shortly after arriving at the hospital, I gave birth to a four-pound precious boy who has been the light of my life ever since.

It was hard in the beginning. I was on welfare, government housing, food stamps, and every other governmental program. I went to college but ended up dropping out twice before I graduated. I've been a single parent for eighteen years now and honestly, I wouldn't change it if I could. I have experienced many ups and downs and the journey of single parenthood hasn't been easy, but it made a real woman out of me. My child has taught me things that couldn't be found in a textbook. He is truly a blessing and I praise God for his life.

The fall of 2013 was when everything changed for us. One evening after work, I was called in to HR and handed my walking papers. After being let go, I immediately filed for unemployment but due to a previous case, I was under some investigation. While under investigation, I had zero income. I still had rent, car note, and other personal bills but no clue as to how I was going to pay them. In a moment of frustration, I cried out to God and asked Him to move quick!!!

He moved, but His direction surprised me. Instead of giving me another job, He taught me how to use what was in my hands. I've always been crafty, so I began making customized bracelets and t-shirts. That business took off rather quickly and provided a stream of income, however, it still wasn't enough. After nine months, I was hired at a hospital working in my field. The job was okay, but I was still unfulfilled. I knew that I was called to be an entrepreneur but I was afraid. A check every two weeks is for sure money, so quitting and taking a chance on myself was scary. I wouldn't do it on my own, so God helped me.

One day, my employer advised that my services were no longer needed. After being "freed" from that job, God advised me that my gifts would make room for me and not to look for another job. I'm happy to testify that I've been a full-time entrepreneur ever since and God has blown our minds. I went from wearing flip flops all year round to having a closet full of nice things. It isn't about the material things though. I've been able to give-back and help others pay their rent and utility bills. God has truly given me beauty for ashes, and I worship Him.

Dear Single Mom,

Your parental status doesn't define you. Odds might be statistically stacked against you, but you were built to defy the odds. I want to encourage you to revisit your dreams, dust them off of the shelf, and get busy working the vision.

Don't use your child/children as an excuse as to why you can't accomplish your goals but, instead, use them as a reason to execute. The choices you make today can destroy generational and familial curses in the future.

You were meant to be a change agent and now it's time for you to truly become the change you want to see.

Alandria Lloyd is a known as the "Change Agent Ambassador" who empowers women to arise from a pit of pain and walk boldly in their God-given power and authority.

She had to become a Change AGENT in own life after experiencing great trials. By the age of sixteen, Alandria had buried two children. After losing her children, she feared losing her mind, but in the midst of darkness, sadness, and despair, she found God.

She is also a serial entrepreneur, award-winning, best-selling author, award-winning philanthropist, and book coach.

She is the author of:

- *Change AGENT: The Missing Piece*
- *While I'm Waiting (Devotional for Single Women)*
- *Girl Power Uncensored (co-author)*
- *Dear Young Woman Vol 1*

- *I'm Coming Out: Overcoming Everything that Tried to Overtake Me*
- *Dear Young Woman Vol 2*
- *Dear Single Mom: You Were Built to Defy the Odds*

Alandria is the owner of a book publishing company, The Writer's Block LLC. The Writer's Block assists aspiring authors by teaching them how to write their book in record breaking speed and become published authors without breaking the bank.

She offers online writing classes, book consultations, book coaching cohorts, publishing packages, and more. To contact Alandria, you can send an email to info@thewritersblockllc.com or visit bit.ly/TWBclarity to schedule a free call.

The authors would like to THANK YOU for supporting and purchasing a copy of this book. If you were encouraged by the stories, please leave a 5-star review on our Amazon page.

If you have an idea for a book or would like to compile an anthology of your own, please visit bit.ly/TWBclarity to schedule a free call to discuss your vision.

The Writer's Block LLC would love to help bring your vision to pass.

Made in the USA
Columbia, SC
25 January 2021